T0082501

ICe CReaM
of the Mind

Kathy V. Kuzma

authorHOUSE®

AuthorHouse™
1663 Liberty Drive
Bloomington, IN 47403
www.authorhouse.com
Phone: 1 (800) 839-8640

Published by AuthorHouse 01/18/2018

ISBN: 978-1-5462-2436-5 (sc)
ISBN: 978-1-5462-2435-8 (e)

Dedication

I dedicate my book to my late sister-in-law, Connie Lucas. She was an artist who used vivid colors to reflect her life and creative style. Connie's images are much like my poetry. They are portraits of imagination.

Contents

The Last Gallery
(in loving memory of Connie)

Frame her on the stairs
A lady with no shoes
Holding on
She was a work of art
Like her vivid colors,
    dreams and beauty
She is now what she painted,
Confined forever in my mind

She would climb upwards
To her last goodbye,
Leaving her treasures behind
Like lost shoes
    and lost time
But her vibrant visions
Were imprinted on the steps
    and in my heart

The Mark

A dent in the wall
Now repaired
An invisible bandaid
Like an image
Of leaves
On a bare tree
A dying eye
Opaque – once blue
A whistled note
    Listening still
They leave a mark
A kiss still felt
Ice cream of the mind
All tattooed inside

Secret Ingestion

Poems eat chaos
And leave the crumbs
Pieces to follow
To find your way
Images chewed
Swallowed whole
Tasty tidbits
On the tongue
Secrets dribbled
And wiped away
Turmoil digested
Replete for the day
Ready for another
   Poetic buffet

Panoptic Perfection

Equilibrium
Wholeness
Symmetrical order
The intricate wires
In perfect form
A harmonious flow
Everything just so

No matter the chaos
In the outer world
The inner vision
Is always concrete
Just straighten
The picture
Stability complete

Alignment

Instinct made her decide
Align what was inclined
All packed and ready
To bolster the unsteady

She was unprepared
For horizontal tilting
Slanting sideways
A declining phase

Vertical and straight
It was her job to make life level
Pull the drooping shadow upright
Focus the oblique light

Her impulse saw it all
A crooked picture falling
She smoothed the fragile breath
But could not unbend death

White Canvas

Blank landscape
A nothing scene
White windows
Without eyelashes
Naked in extreme

Brushstrokes
With our eyes
Blue in morning skies
Brown as coffee beans
Forrest foliage greens

We paint the
Undressed view
Add pigment
To the white
Enhance life
Through our sight

Slip & Slide

Water dripped
Randomly
A race
To keep life dry
A clueless ride
On a paper slide

Wish you could
Slip... float away
But sometimes
It's best
Just to mop
Up the day

Green Summer

The grassy hilltop
With fresh haircuts
Soft and spongy
In the sunburned heat
A somersault summer
With barefoot feet

The rolling wheel
Of youth and time
Closed its eyes
Drank the scene
Tumbled downward
And became the green

Recycle

Sheets of paper
Stream past
Changing lives
Like windows
Open and close
Rustling reams
Ripple in the wind
And then pause
Falter and die

Life whisks
Them away
As the rolls
Unwind
And new lines
Appear
To be rehearsed
Recycled
And rewound

Until no more
Words
Are found

Lullaby

the sway in the hammock
adjusted to the wind
in musical notes
of chimes on the porch
a soft silence singing
in a small quiet room
with the lights flickering
like the sun
through the trees
a watered down drink
that eases the mind
without the high
and there we lie
in motion
   with the sky

Dark Windows

The light flickers in the room and the black windows close
Like the tunnel up ahead and the closet by the bed
Listen in the dark — hear what is not said
The daylight sometimes falters and brightness makes you blind
Like shiny things that glitter and the exit door you find
They are not always what you want or what you really need
The darkness never lies to you — it only makes you heed
Every sound you hear at night lights an image in your head
Imagination swallows you until you are well fed

Then you finally realize what light and dark might mean
Clear windows give you hope in a bold and vivid scene
But the dark ones get you ready...
   Most of life is unforeseen

The 2nd Floor

The 2nd floor
Beckoned
With guilt
Summoned
Opened
The door

Like an
Abscessed
Tooth
Or the cold sweat
Of knowing
The truth

Run up
The stairs
Bypass it all
Slivers
From wounds
On the 2nd floor

Missing

A portal opens
Fish swim out
They use their fins
To cover your stuff
Hide the objects
And make you doubt

Things disappear
Drift away
You cannot find them
In the invisible sea
But one by one
They float back in

You can only hope
They will stay...

Choice

The journey is short
The water is cold
We dance
As we're told

A wire or string
Will hold you still
Like puppets
Never free

A leaf in the stream
Can float to the sea
Its ability to move
Is the key

Which will you be?

A Slice of Night

Lime green curves snaked the sky
Like jello in a mold
Chunks of cloud-like frosting
Powdered the purple night
Dark chocolate shadows rose

A full moon mystery above
Awakened by the passing day
Stirred with polished stars
A portrait whole and raw
And served to those who saw

Down Below

Stone walls
with cobwebs
Shadows
that vex
and warn
A specter
on the
stair
Monsters
in the mortar
Cold breath
in the air

Basements
and cellars
Old things
now buried
Hidden
and forgotten
Where flowers
never grow
We should not
ever go there
   But...
We all end up
below

In The Wind

Touch the feathered pods
Release the seeds within
Like messages from a child
Passing candid notes
Hoping no one will see
Afraid of what might be
Open hungry mouths
They wait like broken shells
Fill their husks again
With needful bits to share
No rest for fragile things
Secrets with weary wings

Sealed

Folded over
Like an envelope
Sealed and set
Not easily opened
Without a tear or rip
A sciatic nerve
From toe to hip

A sudden turn
Twist or bend
A lock in motion
A time to quit
Read the letter
Sigh and sit

The envelope
Is resting now
An outer body
Where pain
Can hide
What's deep
Inside

Stopgap

The light turned red
Free falling in the lane
As the lazy beam
Turned inward
And created a scene
A field of grain

Stubby stalks
Dressed in orange
Then scarlet
Sunset surrender
From seepage
In the brain

Green glowing globe
Pushed her forward
But for a moment...
Between red and green
Her world was sane

Impulse

Rocking back and forth — hammock swaying
A pendulum of flesh that curves and swerves
There is a time when stillness stops
When the air itself swirls and swells
A span of moments that must take flight
No longer able to suppress the flux
Or dam the river from its flow
The fluid steps do not ebb
And cannot pause for ploys or plans
The urgent scratch upon the door
Must open wide to liberate

The myriad musings of the mind
Cannot be quenched
They just unwind

Satin

So very soft and gentle
Fingers touching life
Smoothing out the patterns
Checkered fluff and fur
Purring in the moment
So short the softened kiss

Now the strokes are taken
Made for other years
Not for tender moments
Just dreams and fantasies
The satin shine of loving
Untouched except for tears

Parts

Multiple pieces
Cut from the whole
Joined together
With invisible string
Each sliced
Equally

The thread
Binds them
But they work
Independently
Without knowing
They are connected

The parts
Claw and scratch
At life
Never realizing
It would be easier
If they just
Held hands

Witch Hunt

Fingers point
Like stiletto heals
They dig
Into the ground
Find the dirt.
Uncover it
But stains
Still abound

High status
With the glitz
Of fashion
Seldom
Look around
But check
Your mirror
Often

Before a witch
Is drowned

Edge of Madness

A mad triangle
Three sided monster
Fighting over lines
Exaggerating length
Diamond studded lies
To emphasize their size

Inside the triangle
The space fought too
Some for the right
Others for the left
The bottom had no clue
All sides were equal
Only the edges knew

Tomorrow's Thunder

Flip
Wake up
Traveling is done
You flew to the sun
Fought spiders
In the trees
Lived on the seas

All completed
In a sleeping phase
What happens
If tomorrow
Never comes?
Do we slumber
Through the
Thunder?

Do we keep on
Roaming
In the jungles
Of the night?
Or rest
In the shade
Til a new world
Is made?

Shadow Dance

The sun had waltzed away
And left its shadow
It skipped into the room
Happy to be free
To cavort and prance
In a sequined cape
The daylight couldn't stay
The darkness danced
Pirouetting on walls
It sketched and etched
Painted prints in gray
A nightly parade
In black brocade
A ghost in a ballet

Fraction

A fraction of yourself
Scrambles
Through the weeds
Down in the tunnels
Under the bridges
Across the tracks
In the streets
Hiding from failure
Looking for peace

Always there
   Waiting
At any moment
When a coin spins
And stands on end
The revolving door
   Stops
And you are stuck

The fraction lives
In the land of
   Luck

The Last Trail

Timid souls tiptoe sideways in the woods
They travel lightly in black and white
Patterns that cross the floor of leaves
Swaying slightly with an invisible load
One that weaves with shadowed trees
Like wavy branches in the rain
And ghostly scenes on a window pane

They carry sadness down the paths
The souls of silenced silhouettes
No voices dance in rippled rhyme
As evening settles through the vines
Footsteps leave their sullen marks
But brooms of fairies sweep away
And all that's left is the light of day

Collision

There is always
A something
It's in the closet
Or under the bed
It ties knots
In shoe laces
And wrinkles
Old faces

Perhaps there's
A nothing
In another place
Where all
Is perfect
No time
Or space

If the two
Collide
Would the
Something
And Nothing
Implode
Then explode?

Poured Imagery

Liquid passion poured
Into a floral cup
Purple petals
Floated to the top
With caramel cream
And mocha mints

Ivory sugar melted
When the spoon
Spattered silver drops
And dripped images
Onto yellow napkins
With turquoise swirls

Her sable eyes
Looked into the cup
Saw sapphire shapes
With ruby rhymes
Her lilac lips parted
And she drank...

Brain Ponder

Brain cells curve
Twist and flicker
A parking lot of
Illumination
Where the lights
Stay on for
Days and nights

Cells ride the wires
Park and wander
Shop the connections
And then return
Filled with gifts
Regenerated neurons
　　To ponder

Solid

A square
Inside a circle
A dot within
Warm and safe
The inner pillow
Of comfort
Where bells
Don't ring

The circle rotates
The square hovers
But the dot
Stays still
Bells outside
A solid space
A quiet place
To hide

Dance Chraay

In between the drops and dreams
The latent rain sprayed dissonance
Scattered lilies and skeletons
Like littered streets and alleyways
Foam and fiber resting in place
Sadness and silence in a tired face

Sprinkled spatter skipped a step
Found the rhythm and synchronized
Organized the conflicted mind
Sang a song of consonance
Danced and twirled in a new ballet
Bouquets and bones no longer stray

The Chase

oozing its way
with blind fingers
merging
with the sighs
and shivers
in the flora
and fauna

the stream ran
it was pursued
by the flow
of Life
the bubbling
zest
of freedom
pure magic
in momentum

Discord

Cymbals came together
As the chair was pulled
Kids playing games
Taunting
Laughing

Like an orchestra
The maestro smiling
A planned symphony
Dissonance
With a downbeat

But the child
On the floor
Was the flat note
A solo out of tune
The crashing sound
Of dignity

It was a discord
That would linger
Long after
The ensemble
Was gone

Cocooned

Turned the handle
Opened
Saw too much
Closed the door
Pushed the bolt
Like setting a clock
Only backwards
Life was locked

The inside
Can't get out
The outside
Can't get in
Stagnant thoughts
Congealed
Rigid reasoning
    Sealed

The Quiet

Tired eyes
   Closed
A long sleep
The days tiptoed
Quiet steps
Walking away

The door closed
   A red door
One that slammed
Without a sound
We all saw it
We all knew

Like seeing ourselves
   A rehearsal
For what's to come
But each time
The red gets darker
The door slams harder

We hear The Quiet
   Coming
When we are tired
And the days
Walk away

WHO

Who are we
Inside?
Shells crack open
Like an egg
What is there?
The mind or soul?
Perhaps the whole

Bodies hold us in
Boundaries of skin
A thin disguise
Zippers closed
All buttoned up
Shoe laces tied
WHO do we hide?

DOLDRUMS

Smooth like jello
Calm as the sea
A moment
Or a week
When the wind stops
A time to be

A halcyon zone
When the sails
Are still
Reflective reason
As you drink
Your fill

Melancholy
Moments
When it all
Makes sense

Guardian

Red floral night light
A small beacon
Frightens monsters
In the hall
Casting shadows
That replicate
Their souls

They retreat
As they face
Themselves...
The horror
Reflected back
In mirrored touch
Is just too much

Scattered

Old age turns
Sideways
Becomes thin
But still
Mends the fence
   Herds the ghosts

They wander
But are contained
Until
One by one
They dig or climb
   And run away

Then the corral
Is empty
Vacant voices
Scatter
Too late
   To matter

perpendicular

A vertical reclines
Pulls the peace
Through a hole
Inside a space
A slumber place

Horizontal now
The hole contracts
It's there we keep
The lines of sleep

Right angles
Up and down
Close the hole
Cradle us
And align the soul

Trauma

Falling in a dream
The eye followed the haze
Black bouncing beads
Swirling in razor rain
Blue conscious circles
With stains of red
Like rubbing your eyes
The colors swirl

Reality racing forward
Foggy thoughts tumble
Clustered nerves resound
Vibrations purr and pounce
Catlike creatures cry
Scratching to be free

A second swivels by
A head filled with pain
Resonance in the brain

little things

inside the outside
a box within a box
a pea under a shell
little nesting dolls
inner parts are small
scatter them
leave them out
forget they are there

keep in disarray
never throw away
in case you didn't know
tiny things grow

Vital Vines

Spreading arms
Entanglements
Vines like roots
Above the ground
Connection found

Until a severance
A cutting space
Leaves you floating
Without a face

Tentacles of touch
Can mean so much
Vines sincere
Don't always appear

Soothing Soup

Darkness
Curving road
White fence
Angry voice
Lost in the night

Swirled together
They made a soup
Stirred with ire
Whipped with angst
Poured with mirth

Inside the fence
The road was straight
It ate the soup
Turned on a light
And closed the gate

Consigned

Wild stripes flew
They soared with squares
The two began to blend
   Lines inside a box
A muffled masquerade
Shuffling sounds
Tiptoed tones
   A tidy little life
But deep set stripes
From lines confined
Though redefined
Were never left behind

Elixir Daze

   Mental melting
   Like cubes of ice
   Slowly dissolving
   In elixir mixtures
   A final repass
   Where thoughts
   Are emptied
   Into a glass

   An entire entity
   Slipping into slumber
   While stealing senses
   Blurring vision
   In a habitual haze
   A fading fugue
   Searching for serenity
   In a revolving maze

It's Complicated

Buttons can be pushed
Some turn on and off
Others are more complicated
Like detonating a bomb
Delicate decisions
Need a mind that is calm

Random poking – pressing
In anger or for spite
Petty indignation
Not knowing all the facts
Impulsive acts in darkness
Can lead to needless acts

One button could be tragic
When we swallow
All that's said
Ignorance and intolerance
Should never be fed

Respect

The chair was uncomfortable
But you sat there til noon
It felt like cement
No support or decor
It made time stretch
Like an endless prayer
Stoic detention
Because you care

So many moments
You have to endure
Remembering how
You've travelled so far
So you sit and submit
In honor or respect
Because...
That's who you are

The Quest
(for all my passengers)

It was dark going and coming
The bodies converged
Piled into an even darker place
And then they were off
Like fish swimming upward
   Taking a breath
But then submerging once again
A small light appeared within

And when they stopped
They found a flicker
That led to illumination
There they swam longer
   Faster
Until it was time to gather
Confine themselves
And find the darkness again

The traveling from dim to dark
Had an in-between
There the lights changed
   One by one
Until their heads were filled
And the darkness was no more

The car carried passengers
   To and from
It might have been a quest
A time to learn
   It was called LIFE

The Slaughter

Electric hammer
Broke the banter
Sealed the silence
With a drink of lead

Heated anger
Chewed and swallowed
Burned the inside
With scripted dread

Beneath the tongue
Words were thrashing,
Bubbling, lashing
But love...
          was dead

Swamp Things

Massive moss covered monsters
Stir in the swarthy swamp
These wetland wonders whisper
As willow trees watch them gyre
Their muddy mouths murmur
Like magicians in a mire

They lash their tongues and tails
In an eerie escapade
Dance in blue-green splendor
And cavort in the glade
The trees see their beauty
  Only humans are afraid

Recalculating

Destination cursed
There was no house
Just a rain soaked field
Filled with weeds
Cattails and reeds

Turn back around
Recalculate
Start over again
But still all wrong
Like a lip synced song

Nothing was real
A delusive memory
False teeth in a jar
What you hoped to see
Had ceased to be

Doorbell

Startled by the sound
Vibrations reverberated
Throughout the house
And deep within

Fortuitous fortunes
Or deadly disguises
The door awaited
With the beleaguered bell

They became one
Door and bell
Pulsating like a heart
Open...
    And tear them apart

Waiting

Fingers firmly tapping
An offbeat rhythm
Impatience
Hurried impertinence
An obstinate appeal
To move quicker

A flurry of life
Gone while we wait
A blank interval
Wasted space
Fingers grasping air
Nothing's there

Searching

Going backward...
In the corner of a room
eyes followed the others
Chaotic creatures
blindly searching

The eyes wondered
the purpose
Quiet stillness was better
Observing
Searching for meaning

Constant questions
Why the silence?
They had no clue
Perhaps her eyes
saw more than they
    knew

Rage

His fists were tight
They would not open
Like lips
That keep secrets
Emotions too hot
Or too cold to hold

Closed like his mind
Empty hands
Clenched in hate
A festering anger
Toxic rage
Evil in a cage

Detour

A slanted swerving slide
Down contorted curves
As straightness bent
Time twisted and tangled
Words wavered
Thoughts inclined
And moments intertwined

Days shifted sideways
At alternating angles
As memory veered
Not slowly — but sharply
It crashed into reality
And crumpled inside
A mindless ride

puddle wonder

Footsteps in the rain
Splashing through a puddle
Never looking down
Submerged in thought
No fantasy or wonder
Not even hearing thunder

The puddle may be deep
Who knows what's there
A portal or dimension
A world beneath our own
Use your mind to see
Imagine what could be

Concoction

Falling in a dream
The eye followed the haze
Black bouncing beads
Swirling in razor rain
Blue conscious circles
With stains of red
Like rubbing your eyes
The colors swirl

Reality racing forward
Foggy thoughts tumble
Clustered nerves resound
Vibrations purr and pounce
Catlike creatures cry
Scratching to be free

A second swivels by
A head filled with pain
Resonance in the brain

Inside Out

Everything is inside out
Skirts and shirts
Leggings and pants
It takes so much longer
To right the wrong
Like matching socks
That don't belong

It may not matter
When it comes to clothes
But emotions are hidden
Inside the heart
When they should be open
Shared with honesty
So we all can see

Switch things around
No secret agendas
Games that we play
Turn inside out
And keep it that way

The Purge

It wound around
   Like a tangled hose
And chewed away
   Bits of yesterday

Families and friends
   Faces and time
Purging life's poem
   Of internal rhyme

A process of forgetting
   What was left behind
It ate the memories...
   Perhaps it was kind

Nightlight

Clouds veiled the moon
Like wispy curtains
Still able to see
But not clearly
The light was dim
The world was asleep
It forgot to leave
   The light on

In the window of life
The curtains are shrouds
Nature's disasters
Mankind's violence
Eyes and minds dulled
Like foggy mirrors

Someone...
   Turn the light back on

Compassion

Wing or tail
Paw or beak
What kind of human
Could look away
Or hurt the weak?
Tender moments
With tiny feet
Fur and feathers
Define your soul
Who we are
Is what they see
Let them be

Sequel

A scraping sensation
Like sandpaper
It was deafening
Although intermittent
The day was awake

It was trying to escape
Like an unfinished poem
It needed a sequel
A series
With previews

It could stop
But the world moves on
Scratching and clawing
    Until
Like a balloon...
    It will pop

Glass Bridge

Walking the Bridge
Like life on glass
So much to see
But fear makes us small
We are ants on a wall

The Bridge redefines
As we cross the abyss
Some gaze up
Others glare down
Like bugs we crawl
Trying not to fall

The Dark Side

Into the mirror
To the other side
The reflective reverse
Of what we hide

Clarity concealed
Behind the shine
The darkness dwells
On a borderline

Don't wake the evil
Or delve too deep
Stay in front of the mirror
Let the shadows sleep

Hungry Closet

Like vacant houses
The empty closet
Wanted some stuff
It was voracious
Never had enough

Soon there were gadgets
Kleenex and napkins
Collars for dogs
Catnip for cats
Clothespins leftover
From long ago days
Vases once used
For fresh bouquets

Then it was happy
And there was no clue
What wonders
You'd forgotten
But the closet knew

Travelers

Dream episodes
The dizzy dance
Of projected images
On closed eyelids
Rare acts of reason
In fields of folly
As a beggar or king
The tales begin

We travel in drama
In the blush of youth
And wrinkles of age
In an invisible cloak
A slumbering specter
In florid flair
But...
We're not really there

Clear Ride

The weeks ran dry
A haze of hollow days
A muddied mental ride
Choked inside

But in the water
Ripples sailed on
A smooth transition
From day to night
Halos of sun followed
Guardians of reflection
Clear perfection

Like the stream
Let the current
Guide your boat
Just float…

The Middle

Earth cracked
Above and below
Squeezed in the middle
We huddle in fear
Like rabbits in a storm
Drenched - leveled
And burned away
It's nature's way

But mankind's hate
And the threat of war
Crushes the middle
Even more…

Sleepers

It rained last night
It smelled like blood
Sadness sprinkled
Drizzled dread
Some asleep
While others drown
Evil forces all around

A sapient being
Someone sane
Must wake the sleepers
   And stop the rain

Flare Up

Scales fell like dragons' teeth
Sharp and ragged one by one
Leaving remnants red and raw
Injuries that ooze and sting
Blisters burned the naked skin
A fire raged deep within
A wound inflicted in the past
Festered like a septic sore
An open book caught the flame
Turned the pages – found the cure
A simple fix we all should know
The remedy? Just let go!

Frisson

Ice cream visions
In a chilling mist
Paraded in bubbles
With a frigid twist

The tingling flutter
Like chocolate rain
Dripped dramatically
In a cerebral stain

A brain freeze surged
In a biting blast
Make it last
The rush won't last

Eye Lids

What do you see
When your eyes are closed?
Black holes of nothing?
An empty mind?
Internally blind?

Or an emerging poem
Rich with rhymes
Oceans at sunset
A fleet of ships
Peppermint lips

Lemon wedges on a plate
Cinnamon sand on your feet
A battlefield of raging red
The chartreuse dress in a store
A plethora of scenes to explore

Turn on the light
Behind your eyes
    There's so much more

Unplugged

So quiet
Sitting alone
Like a painting
Abstract
Colorful
Fascinating
But all wrong

She was reserved
A vacuum unplugged
Filled with passion
So much volume
A capacity for more
But no one checked inside
No one plugged her in

If they did…

They would find a poet
A beautiful mind
Looking outward
At those who stared
Heads so very small
Shrinking before her
Until they were gone

Flourish

Raspberry remnants roll back the years
Peel away layers of lavender
Watermelon waves of juicy bites
The shadowy shade of street lights

All on a night that curves and sways
Like roads of dusty dreams
Heat on the bricks of a place called home
Revelations ripe for a poem

Turn the lantern and see the shapes
Listen to nature as it sings
Eat your memories under the moon
Smell the wind wafting perfume

Life is in bloom!

Dark Daze

So very dark
Creeping quietly
Fumbling, stumbling
Naked and afraid
Then it began
That chill sliding down
In fear and dread
Like the walking dead

A rush — a dizzy daze
Of swirling disarray
As the door opens wide
Swallowing you inside
Now a bell rings
Your head spins
Life is cruel
Back to school

Bear Button

The button was once a nose
A brown bear wore it
Then recycled to the button bin
Bouncing between a burly fastener
And a dainty satin covered clasp
The bear nose asked
For another task

Reincarnations arose
All from a bear button nose
It closed the gaps
Such a simple thing
Held together with string
Our world could do
With a button or two

Screed

The rant began in anger
Toxic words flowed
As the bystanders hid
Their yellow umbrellas
Made a shield
From the verbal bullets

The tirade shot red blanks
The screed was just as hollow
Hitting the crowd
But bouncing harmlessly
Into orange puddles
Diluted bubbles

The assault continued
But the rain washed away
The endless blather
An epilogue didn't matter
Banal babble exposed
The umbrellas closed

Sole Full

Smiling sidewalks sang
A tune of footsteps
The soft slippers of age
A high heeled poke
Sandals flopping
Children hopping
Paw pads too
Heated happiness
Shining through

The cement
Felt the hurry
The worry
A warm sense of life
Passing to
Or from
Caresses from laces
Feet on walkways' faces
Sole embraces

Soto Voce

Embarrassing moments
Came alive
They mumbled in soft voices
Recalling every detail
Of choking fluster
Secrets too mortifying
To mention
Demanded attention

The murmurs resurfaced
Blushing beads of sweat
Dripped into open boxes
That were once sealed
Those hushed horrors
Never really healed

Make them close
So no one knows

Untruths

Not quite the truth?
Then what could it be?
A fable or a myth?
A simple fantasy?
Our words are history

Fake feelings
Are even worse
We believe because
We must
And give because
We trust

But truths in disguise
If we are wise
Are just called
　Lies

Uneven

Wobbling in the chair on broken tiled floor
While the crooked picture tilted even more
The curtain was an inch too short
Mismatched socks jumbled in the drawer
Things are not the way they should be
Blue velvet skies with floral tapestry

Uneven patterns placed in tattered piles
A motley mess of mangled tangled miles
The world is floating in a shattered ship
And drowning in a hurricane
The sky is now the sea
Nothing is as it could be

Breathing Fire

The rhythm of the chest
Much like a song
Smooth as a heart beat
A companion so long
It rises and falls
Bellows stoking fire
In rage love and fear
The reason we are here

Objects never stop
As long as plugs and batteries
Keep the power up
But when the human heart
Turns the volume off
We turn it on inside
Where memories reside

Come What May

The elephant
Materialized
Around the corner
The car stalled
It was a moment
Startled inanity
A time to ponder
Your sanity

Like awakening
After surgery
Too groggy
To care
Or understand
But aware
Strangeness
Was in the air

Then fish
Fell from the sky
There was no reason
Slippery and wet
An illusion perhaps
But maybe not
And why was it
So hot?

Shake your head
And sigh
One more road
To ride
Though it was
Melting up ahead
And your feet
Just turned to lead

Ahhh...come what may
    Another day

Enter

Open the gate
Stumble and fall
Belongings are heavy
Not easy to haul

Like beggars
Pushing their carts
Filled with junk
Hoarded objects
Needful things
All the baggage
That money brings

No longer useful
Like dripping
Ice cream
Melting in heat
Too late to eat

NOTHING
Goes with you
Through the gate
Not envy spite
Prejudice or hate

Poetic Pottery

Mold the clay into a shape
Keep it moist and pliable
Sculpt with desire
Passion and ire
Like kissing with ardor
Or strangling a lover
You're bound to uncover
Seeds in a flower

Allow it to dry
Then chisel away
A little here and there
Imagination's your guide
Thoughts and clay collide
Let it be
   And step aside

Mugged

The ambush
Attacked the back
Struck the arms
And seized the neck
Like rubber bands
Wound around skin
Someone let
A stranger in

It was not welcome
It was not polite
The intruder
Sought to enter
To invade
A restful night

It struggled
With the body
Barbed wire
Winding slow
It stole
An evening's
Slumber

But like a
Frightened felon
It finally…
Let go

Ache

Bones in cold slumber
Awaken and speak
A tale of waiting
In blankets of muscle
Protected in sleep
Sparks from embers
Smolder and burn
Tendons tremble
Whisper and weep
Fortress of fire
But the yearning
　　Too deep

Secret Sailing

In just minutes
A voyage
Around the world
Slow motion
Drawn out
Inside the
   Brain

The bell rings
Somewhere
In your head
A distant call
Your ship sails
Everywhere…
   But here

No one knows
You travelled
A mental journey
In 5 minutes
The sea is yours
As time passes
Between classes

Credence

Three eyed beasts
Green walking twigs
A box of spiny things
Purple porcupines
With wings
Few can see them
Only those who perceive
And believe

They can hear the whispers
Through the trees
See the sparks
From the evening breeze
Enchantment of the
Mind
Letting imagination
Unwind

Perhaps not really there
But stories become real
And the world seems
More alive
If magic can survive

The Shelf

The top shelf
Was empty
It once held
Knick knacks
   But
Like umbrellas
Only used
In the rain
Or to keep us
   Sane

Porcelain reminders
Of what we
Leave behind
We take them out
   To marvel
A bauble to hold
As we grow old

   But
Now the shelf
Is bare…
   Because
We are not
   There

Crushed Connection

Books were scattered
Images cracked
Words were flying
As the letters snapped

Speech was altered
Voices faltered
Symbols fled
Language was dead

Tongues were useless
They shrank in size
No more reading
We lost our eyes

Nothing to say
Nothing to see
When we crush
Expression
We cease to be

Off the Path

As you age
    A memory
Must be found
On the third floor
No stairs going up
Many going down
Ones that go nowhere
Even those that wander
Leaving you outside
    On a path
You are late
So you wait
Shaken — tossed
    And lost

The fog will clear
The room will appear
But now you
Disappear
    Or perhaps...
You were never
    Here

The Red Basket

FIlled — on fire
Never consumed
No ashes
No debris
A weave of restraint
Constant containment
Stasis in red
A basket not fed

Piled to the rim
A thirst never quenched
Borders and edges
Confinement refined
A burning addiction
Stored and repressed
Fibers in flame
Waiting for rain

Full

The heart is hungry
It craves...

A classic story
Poetic imagery
Artistic beauty
Musical medley
Athletic prowess
One more kiss
Extra strength
Second wind
One more try
One last breath

We are not empty
We are not dead
Just keep us fed

Inflation

Condescending smirks
Float above the rest
Like helium
In balloons
Green and grinning
Arrogance
Inflated with conceit
Imposing pride
Sucks the air
A high pitched voice
Then cries
The tiny sound
Leaks lies

Balloons
Are sometimes
Overblown
And deflate
With too much
Weight

The Backdoor

Soft slippery hands
Slide into pockets
Steal secrets
Strange keys
That open backdoors
Interiors filled with riddles
Disguises on display

Revelations in mirrors
As masks conceal
The Self
Check the doors
For pretense
New faces
Are on the shelf

Self-Stick

Clear tape
Wraps us up
Sticky reminders
It's time to stop
Adhesive goo
Of a gorilla day
Puts things in order
And makes them
     Stay

Glue the bottom
To the top
Bend the edges
Curl them up
You're in the
Middle
Plastered tight
You can finally
Say goodnight

Stuck at last
The day
Has crashed

Heart of Darkness

Frigid freeze
Chalkboard screech
Shivering in sleep
Such tiny trembles
Trip us up
Tiptoes in the night

Cringe and cower
Sweaty palms
The icy trickle
Down one's back
The ashen face
Of fear

The horror
Is not just
In your dreams
Wake up
The nightmare
Is everywhere

persuasion

In the crowd
One was red
The rest were
White
The color diffused
Contagion spread
The group turned red

In the crowd
The red turned
White
The color was drained
Depleted of tone
The bloom was spent
With discontent

The blush of life
Like fresco fire
Can bleed
And inspire
But the hollow mind
Travels just the same
In the social game

Things

Bought
Never sold
A tent sale
Junk
Accumulations
Distractions
Piled high in a shed
Visions in your head

Tin signs and toys
Tractors and scythes
Rust and ruin
Dying in the sun
Collected – not used
Like red hats
And silk ties
Do they matter
After your demise?

Green

The earth was black coffee
Fresh — just brewed
The smell of morning
Wafting and waking
The upturned stalks
To make them see
Wonders of the day
Creatures crawling within
Underneath its skin

The grass parted
Long enough
Between the blades
To see the marvels
Gather travel and toil
Life beneath the soil
Fluorescent and serene
Animation in green
    All unseen

Deep Sleep

Gliding guilt free
In golden lands
Sweeping webs
And dust away
Sinking deeper
You cannot stay

Every layer
Pulls you in
Down the ladder
To your secret cave
So very deep
Like an early grave

From wide awake
To level four
And then...
Nothing more

Red Beam

(for my teacher friends)

Out of control
Out of paper
Grasp an idea
Throw it wide
Hope it lands
In someone's lap
Ignite their brain
Before you snap

So many eyes
None on you
A magic act
To trap their minds
Make them see
Red from black
Stir their senses
Bring color back

One kindled soul
Eyes now wide
Grasps more than red
Scarlet wisdom
Blooms in her head
It takes just one
To transfer the beam
Spark and inflame
A colorless dream

Forte

The strength of life
Falls slowly
As we climb
Unless we carry it
In forms or fugues
Passion fed
It will thrive
Keeping us alive

A driving force
Like lightning
A backbone
To your spine
Shockwaves
To the brain
A life stain
That keeps us
   Sane

Bouquet

Behind the fence
Close to the field
Something moved
Like floral curtains
Swaying in wind
Tangible truths
Just barely there
A breath of air

Violets and daisies
Trying to speak
Hiding in shadows
Waiting for humans
To go away
   A reminder
   A bouquet
That nature will stay

The Stage

Zebra stripes
On criss cross gray
Dots of silver
Like tinseled toys
    India ink
Swirled and mixed
A scene so bold
With a tinge of gold

Usher in songs
Of frogs and breeze
Cue the glowing
Lightening bugs
Now the gold is full
    And finite
A catharsis on stage
    A perfect night

Last Days

The moments
In between
Like a zippered
Pocket
Contain
Some peace

There we can
Settle with
Things we love
The faraway
Thunder
Not yet here

Short but happy
That time
And space
A tied
Shoe lace
In the final race

The Bucket

Floating
Like a summer day
A hammock swaying
Berry picking
The bucket full
Looking back
We sailed
Spontaneous
Endless

The hill was ours
Time indulged us
There was no list
No hasty hustle
The rapid race
Had not begun
The bucket full
    Of berries
Not regret
    Not yet...

Transference

Painted portals
Take your hand
Meld and merge
To understand
Suck your substance
From reality
Transcend your mind
As paint and you
    Are intertwined

The colors blend
As they dry
Smear and stain
In a raucous sky
Until at last
You are inside
Now others stare
    And see you there

Pillow Talk

Soft like sifted flour
A restful contented cradle
To soothe a baffling dream
A transport to tomorrow
Respite from misgivings
In white-out heavy cream

Careful cushioned defenders
Sew up an unraveled seam
Renewal from the worry
Peace from the fury
Perfect positioned pillows
Comfort…
    When we scream

Sentient Bond

Room darkening
In turquoise blue
Silver grommets
Glide past the view

Through reflective glass
The drapes have seen
Symbiotic partners
In a world between

The inside domain
And the outside mist
Fabric and vistas
   Coexist

Frenzy Free

Wild random intensity
Settles in the cracks
Drips down
Like spilled coffee
Diluted as it seeps
Slowly descending
Transforming

Limp and languid
Immobile in the transfer
No longer fluid frenzy
But altered anxiety
Sleeping soundly
In catatonic descent
Finally... content

Spaces

Mingling
Alone
Yet surrounded
All the voices
Sound like one
So many lights
They all burn
In unison

One light is out
A candle
With no wick
An umbrella
Over the day
Walk in the spaces
Between the luster
And sneak away

The Last Image
(in memory of my dear friend Bernie Pernia)

The blanket was thin
Way too short
Like life spans
The chair seemed to shrink
As did the occupant
   A blinding sight

Remainders of what was
Just a shallow shape
Now waiting for the end
Stoic searching
   In a dying light

Only a hand held on
Tightly clutching warmth
Such a contrast
Vitality to frailty
Holding onto life
   In that good night

POTLUCK

A short repast
Of curious cuisine
Pass the possibilities
Chew the chances
Digest the desire
All was consumed
Nothing left over

It was the delicacies
That they ate
Like dilemmas
Disappointments
And dreams

The meal was bitter
Dessert sweet
Problems solved
Dinner complete

Dust in Time

A flurry of dust snuck in
It settled down
Like children after play
It nestled in corners
And fell asleep
Quiet sedation soon spread

Tranquil but tenacious
The gray particles prevailed
Placing a shroud of shadows
In the once clean abode
Dreary powder finally spoke
As sun beams found the source

Life is filled with disarray
Time and dust…wiped away

Nocturnal High

There was a citrus moon
In a MilkyWay sky
It was a night of confection
When the air tasted sweet
Stars were lampposts
While we played in the heat
Moving through molasses
On a Starburst street

Eating laughter like candy
No desire to stop
It was an evening dessert
That swallowed the dark
Like a chocolate drop

A sugar high
After a lemon day
Wish those assorted flavors
Would stay

Taut

The knot was ready to bind again
It wedged its fibers in unyielding arms
Folding fabric in straining fists
Stretching strands and holding tight

Fading fingers made it twist
Embedded colors laid to rest
Strangled secrets left inside
Forever hidden within the core
Shrouded memories...
Tied once more

Mi Casa

Domicile doubts
Nomadic nerves
In the blush of youth
Moving in sweat
Heavy and harried
A turbulent task

Persistent panic
To find a nest
That stable brick
Safe sheltered shield
With smooth steps
That greet and guide

Rich colors hide
The scars on walls
Masking lives
Who came before
Move in and meld
   You are
   Home

EMPTY

Picked the tulips in spite
Threw them in the road
Did not ruin the inside
But ripped the sky and moon
Torrential fever raging
Tied by rubber bands
Stretched until broken
Only slivers in a hand
Not by wooden fixtures
But a space left behind
Trouble in the garden
A gap in the soul
A scattering of petals
Only silence in a hole

Paper Trails

A calendar on the table
Flat and stationary
   Spotless
Except for boxed boundaries
And black digits
   Ready
Gateways to gardens
Tucked away — in bloom
Or gray stones
To balance or barter

Open passages
Written roads
But easily erased
   Detoured
Blank nothings
Once more

Gone days
Wiped away
Along with people
   Penciled in
     And
   Penciled out

Memory Foam

The chevron rug
Never moved
But it was soft
Calloused feet awoke
Shuffled sideways
The zig zag dance
   Happy soles

It was a day
Sunshine and concrete
Climbing trees
Toes holding on
Feeling the branches
The heat on cement
   Touching earth

The rug absorbs
Retains the joy
Pleased that feet
Are free
The way all things
   Should be

Tilt

Breathing was so easy
Yet the surface overflows
Liquid running like lava
Not hot but cold

Empty as a shadow
Drained of glow and hue
A voice without inflection
Steady but subdued

A river running sideways
Tilted in the rain
Everything is backwards
People are insane

Place them on the mantel
Rearrange the dusty mess
Turn the picture sideways
Wipe away the stress

Conjure up a mantra
One you think will last
Breathe again and listen
Perhaps this will pass...

The Summons

Frames on the wall
   Portraits
Black fur hats
Blankets of yarn
They sat for years
Glowing – calling
The room spoke too
In rustic brown

They waited for hands
Soft caresses
Warmth from a presence
The flesh colored beings
Those who understood
Objects come alive
   Listen
They are orators
   of the past

Shuffle

Fed the demons
Crossed the path
Closed the gate
Red turned white
Moved the pictures
Back and forth
Like marbles falling
In the night

Shifting patterns
Changing lanes
Missed the traffic
Blocked just one
Turned the corner
Nothing there
Like swept spiders
Webs...not spun

FLAMES

Silk robes of radiant red
In a black room
Flames lapping the walls
A white chair slid into place
As a single light turned on
She saw it in the window
A glimpse inside
She wondered
Was the chair for her?
Could she sit and rest?
Would her darkness sleep?
Could memories burn?
The robes drew her in
She sat
At peace
The light
Switched
Off

Cannibals

Mental menus
   Feast away
Devour our minds
Only fingerprints
   Stay

Nibble beliefs
Gnaw on brains
Drink our dreams
Not much remains

Monsters consume
   Always fed
Look familiar?
   They're inside
      our head

Spirit World

Tales have morals
Lessons to heed
Turn the stone over
Find the right key
Old letters in walls
Ghosts walking halls

They all have a message
Threads left behind
Blood on clothing
Red streaks in the sky
But clues have no meaning
When the world runs awry

Life deals with mysteries
Magic and myths
Shamans and wizards
Know what is true
Find a door in a cornfield
Open…pass through

POLYCHROME

Fluorescent wings
Sapphire seas
Moss covered trees
Eyes – electric blue
Transfusion red
Swirl and sweep
Colors seep

Veins transport
Infuse – instill
Merge and weave
Pulsate inside
A chromatic guide
Hues bleed through
To become YOU

Sordino

The sound of clouds
White creatures
Shaped and shifted
Floating in zephyrs
Albino masses
Music con sordino
Sign language in the sky
Let the world go by

Imaginative filigree
Mirrored in the sea
Speechless harmony

Heavy Stones

Laden loads of labor
Weighty words and ways
Tilt the windmill sideways
Try to see it straight
Look beneath the reason
Like picking up a stone
Cumbersome to carry
Especially all alone
But if there is no answer
Or hands that do not stay
Carry the damn burden
And walk the other way

Tomorrow

Wings of Wildlings
Wipe the day
Erase the filters
Change exposure
From brilliant
To gray

Focus on shadows
Black and white
Closing windows
Like spiders on webs
Sliding down fibers
Shutting out light

Wake tomorrow?
We never know

Gift of Air

An empty balloon
Reluctant to rise
Afraid to soar
One puff
A boost
Just needed air

Like lonely people
And victims of hate
The ill and forgotten
Give prisoners of fate
The gift of momentum
Power to levitate

Chapeau

A gentleman
Like an open door
Waiting with a hat
Tilted just so
Bold and gallant

Knowing that entrance
Goes beyond the opening
A charm for respect
Like a formal act of chivalry
A portal for politeness
Just a chapeau
But it makes one pause…
A prominent symbol
Of pride

Easy Rider

The quiet buzz of nothing
Doors closing like zippered lips
With bits of blank balance

Orderly spaces of time began
No creatures crawling
No monsters in mirrors
White walls rested — as did the rider
No more hunger
As the road lost its appetite
And its mouth closed

Sleeping heartbeat
Dormant days
The taste of easy

Your Turn

The malignancy spread
Not sideways
But straight down the middle
It curved and then paused
To let problems penetrate
And people pass
It assaulted the brain
And pierced the body
Like a silencer on a gun
The shot was not heard
Only felt

It struck some
Subdued others
Distressed many
Leaving the road empty
The leftovers distraught
And what was the cause?
An alternate highway
A change of lanes
A yield sign not seen
Or perhaps…just your turn

Legerdemain

Numbers bounced
Ricocheted
Somersaulted backwards
Almost an invisible touch
A magical mystery
But not quite...

There was a twitch
A slight fold in the eyelid
A quiver of an eyelash
So very insignificant
But it was there
Like a cat's whisker

The lapse lingered
A second of illusion
A reveal from an eye

There are marvels
That could be perfect
But people are not...

Chill

The floor was cold
A crisp apple type bite
Shiver fresh
Creeping to bed
Feet bare and breathing
Time for a frozen night

Not fear of ghosts
But shivery dreams
Always cut in cubes
Chunks of life in ice
Rapid sliding shapes
With chilling themes

The world was numb
With slumbered sighs
That only ate the snow
Passionless lives
Apathetic souls
Sleep with arctic eyes

Decipher

Nimble fingers turned the page
Archaic squiggles
A message there
Perhaps a curse
Warnings to heed
A rant filled with rage

The letters curved
They swirled and swam
Like twisted fences in the sun
Melting symbols dripping wet
Yet bold and strong
Well preserved

Bursts of love never said
Trivial banter famine or feast
Beware or welcome
Inscription now dead

Pages still turning...
Missives unread

Worry Waves

Nervous needful bubbles
Float downward in distress
Restless agitation
Waves of worried wonder
That you can't suppress

It may be tension thunder
Like a ship alone at sea
Uncontrolled and dreadful
Tangled nerves that tremble
    All inside of me...

The Loop

As the hummingbird hovered
The flower enticed
And the nectar flowed
An image in still motion
The same day
Same moment
An emotional sigh
Wrap this in paper
Place in a box
A sequence of senses
A return to what was

Now unwrap the reflection
A loop in perception
Replica in review
And though the same rendering
The depiction is new

Gravitas

It sat on her chest
Heavy
Like dendrites
Reaching outward
Directionless
Something there
   But not really

A beast perhaps?
A forgotten creature
Like a mythical Griffin?
Only less intrusive
   Yet potent

An untold story
Or a poem never shared
A harbored hate
Like a weighty stone
Ingested intentions
Somber secrets
Swallowed too fast

Your Space

Now the time past
Is a space
Once huge
Now small
A ball of yarn
Knitted or crocheted
But eventually frayed

It unravels slowly
Usually by fate
Sometimes by choice
Yarn or thread
Short or long
It is your space
Life's final embrace

Borderline

Delicate balance as it shifted
A waver in the air
Just a thin line for dancing
And a finer one to live
Walk the thread swiftly
Before the knot is made
Continue on sure footed
Your course steady and staid

The colors wink and wander
Your passage pacified
Adaption bends the filament
As you learn to stride and glide
The cord, a constant current
A zipline from birth to the grave
Breathe – enjoy the ride

The Bullet

Drill into the ear and gaze within
Hear the doorbell ring
The dogs bark
The shot
A pulse behind the wall

Vibrations vex the mind
But stir the sanity
Surgical blackness in the cold
Like a bullet to the brain
A dissonant refrain

Peel the skin and hide...
    There
The shrapnel
    Will reside

Open

The bag was transparent
Revealing a pink poem
Soft as the lining of a cocoon
But gleaming like a polished spoon
It would be removed
Cut and pulled out
A little damaged and not well
Time to purge and plunder
Prod and pry
Sad to see it go
Must ponder and prevail
Such vital parts soon dead
    Emptiness instead

Discrete

He was a guileful book of fiction
Always placating in a pleasing sense
He had his dark secrets
Like the safe behind the picture on the wall...
Hidden masks mysteries and mistakes

But his smirking pride projected prudence
Shadowy spiders traced his smile
Tactful vigilance kept them hidden...
He had formed a delusional disguise
Discretion and deceit obscured his lies

Dubious Battle

Crawling through the fields
He tried to pick the right spot
The tulips taunted
As the wrens warbled
And the berries beseeched
It wasn't the fragrant flowers
The lyrical lilt
Or the plump pomes
That made him move on
It was uncertainty
A fear of touching new soil
Perhaps the lure of perfection
Anything that might change his course
Or alter the path
The groove he had made for himself

And so the trench grew deeper
As the bitter sweet berries multiplied
He ate them willingly
   And crawled on...

Duplicity

The underbelly of the clouds reversed
What once was down was up
The roots grew skyward without the soil
Lakes poured down like rain
The rising sun never set
While the night lost its moon
Fish swam in the willow trees
As the flora floated by
Words were useless notes and songs
Forgotten and unsaid
Then mankind shook its empty head

We ate our souls and starved to death
    When ignorance was fed

A Living Fresco

She passed the rose bush
    Or it passed her
The frame remained the same
The flowers never wavered
But her mouth formed a sigh
The landscape was a puzzle
With pieces strewn about
One could almost see a pattern
Like a vision in the rain
A foggy dream at night
You knew where she was going
And hoped she knew the way
But she was frozen in a fresco
Like an atrophied bouquet

Dark Journey

Their world flickered
Just a second,
So the Creatures could awake
Arm themselves with claws and teeth
Battle armor
Below the ground
But some turned backwards
Reversed their steps
They slid or swam
Beneath the war
Not their turn to fight the night
They knew their time would come
When air turned red
Like dragons' breath
The next defense would rise
A journey concealed
Under somber skies

Desperate Dessert

Brown box sturdy
Filled with sand
The color of desire
Like thumbtacks pushed tight
Holding up pictures
In an insomnia night

Sifting through photos
Shuffling a sigh
Eating crumpled paper
Like a dessert for the dead
The box still solid
    Longings unfed

Message Received
(for my mother)

Someone whispered in her ear
Like a hummingbird's touch
Sunbeam on the floor
A tug at the heart
Perhaps not there
Except for that memory
The one she could reach
Like Pebbles in a Sieve
Or Silent Eyes of blue
A song she knew

A voiceless void
In a muted space
A breath
White flowers in snow
Sweet sugar of strength
A pattern of peace
Like coming back home
Where her life was warm
Nothing was heard
But love was transferred

Palaver

A quiet corner to think
Rehearse the words
And then
Like bubbles
Float away
Soft slippery syllables
Dance upon the tongue
Shift and pirouette
Reverse and whirl again
They flow and flip
And sometimes land
Inside the mind of one
Concepts for connection
Thoughts like webs
Are spun

Hidden Holes

Like a foggy recollection
Can't remember a name
A blank stare
Looking through
Always hidden
Barely there

Fragments of futility
Holes in the fabric
Insecurities in her head
She closed the spaces
And sewed her shadows
With invisible thread

The Tower

Climb the steps in the castle
Your footprints disappear
You are not here
The mind wanders upward
Gathers leaves from the ground
Whisper in the forest
Bare trees listen
They know you

No longer climbing
Dreaming in the woods
Watching clouds
A tower in the sky
As the castle floats by

Wilting

The door was waiting
But closed like her heart
Blossoms were dying
As the mouth opened wide
Casting out demons
And spitting black flies
   Defensive replies

Now the door was painted
Fresh once more
But the mouth always ready
To bite and chew
Forgotten darkness
In an empty room
Where flowers can't
   Bloom

Ice Creatures

Voices in the ice
Knock on frozen roofs
Lies that sank in summer
Now trapped beneath the lake
Winter's cold surrender
Keeps them anchored tight
But rumbled curses thunder
And moan to see the light

Water is their prison
But only for a while
Hidden secrets grumble
And thump upon the door
Inmates under ice flows
In a constant state
  Of war

Cloudy Mirrors

Clouded fury rolled into a ball
Blankets of shadows over the head
Smothered reality – almost dead

Turning off faucets that never drip
Silencing voices that try to sing
Still shouting words that stab and sting

Happy in smokey balloons of life
Hazy reflections of the one by your side
  Watching in mirrors,
       as you try to hide

Fading Fibers

Sewing tiny stitches
The needle pauses
Fragile fabric fading
Waiting...

It is a complex cloth
Worn thin and weak
Too much stabbing
Not enough thread
Like words not said

Patching the piece
Persisting too long
A dream gone wrong

Hateful Hearts

Spouting hot lava in livid layers
Piled high in the corner
With news and fire
Ready to rouse a blaze

The mixture of anger
Like a liquid lighter
Rolled out in a field of fate
Igniting power
        pain and sorrow
While burning in venom and hate

The Wall

Inside and out — it was always there
A small corridor insulated and warm
Sturdy brick plaster and paint
Solitude seclusion — alone at last
But a voice hammered on
As the echoes ricocheted
Pummeled with impatience
And bludgeoned in haste
Rattled into reality
No longer encased

Frozen Paths

Footsteps lorn and labored
Walking trails of snow
Dreams that come and go

Plunge your heart in slumber
Talking in your sleep
No one hears you mutter
Secrets dreamers keep

Shadowed lips open
In a timeless photograph
Poised in endless stasis
A frozen fresco half

Forged in a frigid blast
A love we can't remember
A memory that did not last

Ego

The overcoat was too large
It covered many things
People praised its great length,
Its simplicity,
The shiny fabric
            But
What was concealed
    in the pockets?
    in the sleeves?
And most of all
    inside the man?

The facade was almost flawless
Who dared to look beneath?
To pull a thread
Unravel the coat
Prod and pry
And thus reveal the lie

Train Whistle Elegy

Distant traveler
The forlorn wail of life
That far reaching call
Heard between dreams
It wakes us for a moment
Startled by the lament
A doleful cry
Like a lover's goodbye

Someone is crossing
Moving in time
We acknowledge the passing
But sleep on...
Though that dirge
Sings slowly and solemnly
And merges with our mind
A reminder that we are left
Behind

Split Second

Thunder rattled and no one heard
It blustered and clattered in its cage
Confused commotion skipped a beat
Like a murmur inside the heart
A simple second of silent sighs
The blink you feel in your eyes

No one sees that space between
The mirror effects of truths and dares
A pause that lets you stop and think
Gives you the option to moderate
Time surrenders and nullifies
Creating an instant to stabilize

OG Dance (Original Angel)

Close your eyes
There is power in movement
Breathing in and out
Capturing a heart beat
Pulling it out of your chest
Flinging it to the wind

That moment you know the steps
A pulse inside your head
The hammer that forges your soul
Motion finally set free
A cadence of rhythm and rhyme
An egress through space and time

The Crooked Smile

The smirk slid into a side pocket
Hidden in the folds of flannel
It measured the faces
The flicker in the eyes
Ready to explode
Swiftly catching the mouth
No longer willing to hide
Holding it firmly to one side

It was the culmination
With bits of cloth still clinging
Like threads of leering doubt
Fibers of fuzzy fabric
Hanging from the lips
Pockets conceal smug secrets
And sliding smirks will lie
They are smiles... gone awry

Hollow Thirst

Liquid laughter
Mirrored in fluid form
Poured pride
   And
Frigid smiles
   Empty
Like ice cubes in a tray
Gaiety in a glass
   Dissolved

A drink
Of melted mirth

Half

Be careful
   You see the shadow
An outline — a window's fog
Perception cut in half
Like a cracked walnut
Never eaten — just opened
Ready for consumption
A portion pealed — partly there
Broken parts in the dissection
Incomplete...
   Yet still aware

Monsters

Daggers thrust inward – battle scars
Raw and ragged from eating words
Stifled anger and dry eyed stares
Looking out at full moon craze
What else could evil monsters eat?
Checking pulses – perhaps dead?
   Why were they even fed?

But ravenous and hungry wrath
Cannot be stifled stabbed or killed
Devoid of gentle touch or kiss
It burns and turns like tiny blades
And wishful thinking is a curse
The wicked waves roil and rage
And fighting back
   Just makes it worse

Sedation

a cat's whiskers
brushed the daylight
with russet restful hues
soft lips sent a message
blossoms ready to bloom
whispers to the moon

bitter tempests
were soothed by silence
as smothered breezes
blew bits of anger
into a vacuum
with a hint of perfume

Ruby Rapture

There was tinder in her soul
Always glowing in the night
A rare gem that bled
As the heat came alive
Pulsing the purest pearls
Breathing silver jewels
Ripe rare bangles
From a mindful muse

Sweet crimson musings
Dripped from her veins
Flaming darts of wonder
Pierced her rosy rhythm
Gushing ruby petals
Opened in rampant red
Florid freedom
Bloomed...
    Inside her head

Zip Line

The line was taut
  Sliding in whip cream
    Above the anger
      Below the hauteur
        Speeding through words
          Straight and aligned
            Smooth as liqueur

Grabbing fingers
  Plucked and pulled
    Chased the cord
      In cunning deceit
        Aerial refuge
          A slipping mirage
            Evasion complete

Slice

A hole in the window
Taped and secure
Touching the hollow
Freezing the fear

Limping in shadows
Stretching the skin
Tearing the inside
Scraping what's in

Trapped in glass slivers
Fragments of ice
Cold pieces living
In each cutting slice

Solidify

Feathers floating in frigid air
Frozen – never descending
A pause
An interim
When a breath inhales
That moment when you know
The space prolonged

Drops form
Dripping from the hand
Held too high
Never quite reaching
But still melting
Then freezing again
        In mid air
Numb

Captives

A lone gunman
Shot off words
Hitting targets
And exploding
In a verbose
And vibrant voice
A veritable veteran
Of vocabulary

Syrupy bullets
Of sentiment
Discharged
Onto subjects
They lapped it up
Licking their fingers
In desirous delight
Sweet drippings
From the same gun

Shooter
Surrendered
Ammunition
Arrested
Captive audience
Free
The only prisoner
    Was ME

Often
(for my mother)

The table waited
Privileged protection
Lightly covered
Crocheted white cloth
     Warm and cozy
Looking past it
Seeing hands
Needles needful
Vintage masterpiece
     Smiling threads
Sun from the window
Blurred the meaning
Just a table
A shroud in time
     Fingers moving
Reaching backwards
Catch the moment
Love in fibers
Cotton flashback
See the image
     Often...

Below

Bitter the vines that swept the land
Tangled roots in concrete slabs
Pushing entrails through the cracks
Straining upwards in retrospect
Memories plowed under the ground
Like buried treasures to be found

Far below the muddied clouds
Secrets spoke in soliloquies
Rallied forth and spoke in rhyme
Stones and creatures moved aside
Let them pass arise and shriek
Muffled mouths now could speak

Calling

Hidden in the trees the voice sang
Faint at first with strings of silk
Laden with lyrics too soft to hear
But floating in silver tones of steel
Hardened and heavy the lines obscure

Curled and swirled like smoke filled air
Notes rained down and clawed the earth
Changed the pattern...called a name
Trebled silence unearthed and free
A dying song in a constant flame

Circles

Curves and edges tossed about
As quickly as a detoured road
Not ready for that roundabout
The slipping feeling of lost control
Whirling around like a playground twirl
Spinning in circles in blurred release
Hanging on with accepting arms
Clinging to something solid and safe
But wishing to fling into the air
Releasing it all and letting go
Not caring how or where I land
Sliding on the graveled ground
Knees and elbows covered in blood
Future scars to summon the past

Circles stop when you are free
So happy to finally embrace and know
But wish I had jumped... long ago

Blind

Anxious eyes dart and fret
Irregular rhythm in mindless sight
Hiding in shelters under the bridge
Locking the door while windows close
Sweating in blankets that cover the head
Timid glances dance in dreams
Too fearful to enter
Too alive to be dead

Then the dread dimmed its light
Tilted pictures became straight
Nothing there for eyes to fear
Dust and devils cleared away
Melted into sullied air
Eyes now open – as well as doors
Too calm to leave
Too placid to care

Liquify

rolling like mercury
    in silver gloss
wine running down a chin
tears in an empty
    darkened room
goodbyes uttered too soon

swirling water down the drain
the sun swallowed
    by the sea
diluted minds will surely drown
    in floods of apathy

purple

Circular veins formed
Curled around the fence
Undulated through the fields
And swirled through the water
The weeds snagged them
Trying to impede their passage
Like hands warding off a foe
But the purple progression advanced
Stopping only to listen
To feel the pulse of the earth
And hear the chatter of the roots
The seeds beneath the soil

There was much to learn
Much to grasp
Down below
In the sleeping ground
So new to the creeping fingers
Of creatures from afar
There must be peace — if not above
Then somewhere deep within
The dormant slumber of the dirt
Would awaken in the spring
The purple explorers waited...
Hoping to keep tranquility in

Blank

The white paper flattened
afraid of ripe reprisals
The weary rapid writing
of worry and regret
Waiting for the scripting
against its unlined chest

Always poked and prodded
by the pen of fear and doubt
But this time it was pardoned
a reprieve from discontent
Like stifled troubled voices
no composing had occurred

Peace provided stasis
   and never said a word

Flash

Reflected in the window in the dark
An echo of a moment
It flashed inside the mind
Like fireflies at night

Its brevity enhanced its luster
A cache of recollections
Strung like pearls in silent slumber
Awakened now at last

The surge was swift and haunting
Memories still seen in glass
No use hiding reminiscence
It all comes back too fast

The Door

It gradually came into focus
Green and gray
Sprouting from the ground
A singular portal
A visible entry...or exit
Solitary gateway
Just a door In space
An aperture in time
But there is no doubt
We can go in...
or let IT come out

Diversion

The eyes told us to hurry
Create a tale of distraction
One with valleys and hilltops
A journey filled with flurry

A fortune of grassy knolls
Projected on sable scenes
Cobalt brilliance of bluebirds
Decadence without controls

Then the eyes could surrender
Not focus on the world
Find a place of comfort
An interim of private splendor

The Day

TODAY was endless in the evening
IT took its shoes off...sighing
Tension caked on the souls
Pensive plodding through the crowds
Tracks of furtive chances
Emotions on overload
Walking inside the masses
Knowing their pace and tread
So many in need of compassion
Footsteps no longer dancing
No wonder the day is dead

Inquiry

The door was open just a crack
It let the light filter through
It curved – just peeking in
Waiting like a crouching beast

The darkened hall saw it come
Heard the crackle of the heat
Felt the fire of its breath
It shivered in delight

But the door then closed
The fervor quenched
Warmth had never settled in
Love moved on...to seek again

Ten

Numbers like a song
Find their harmony
The perfect tone and pitch
Chalk upon a blackboard
Forming lullabies
A verse of curving symbols
Counting constantly

One will create a memory
A poem in reverse
Digits – like a diagram
A soothing melody
Ten – so round and even
A chorus whole and free
A muse in stability

Outside

turquoise skies
infusing pigments
of bygone spring
raspberry sunsets
elixir in liquid dreams
visage blended
a concoction of beauty

longing to have
the outside
   in

Silence

The spaces in between words
Became larger thicker darker
Until they echoed in the corridor
Trapped there
Waiting for the bold type to appear
Letters in tight formation
Like birds on a wire
Notes on a staff

But windows never opened
And the doors remained shut
The birds flew away
And the music stopped

One O'Clock

A tire
Hung from a tree
A llama
Alone in a field
Sparrows
Saved from a fall
A hummingbird
Perched on a hand
Whistles
Still heard in the wind
Loved ones
Silenced too soon
Inspiration for verse
Images so diverse

There isn't a scene
Object or thought
That cannot be bought
Not with wealth
But with the mind
Close your eyes
See the conception
It appears in your head
One o'clock
And the muse
   Is fed

Word Holes

In a deep well
   We sink
Not a new dimension
Or a 3D hologram
But a paper page
Written words
With cryptic tales
We dive
Find holes
They lead us on
Words swim free
   And so do we

COMPLETE

(For Barbara Saski Lewis
Now, I can have end punctuation)

The curl on her forehead
blew backward.
You could see her face.
One eye drooped.
The rosy blush
made her glow.
And someone said
she was beautiful.

A scribbled design,
never one to be bold.
She painted by number
from one to seventy
inside her frame.
The digits reversed,
faded or flowed,
but her painting sold.

And, indeed,
she felt beautiful!

"There are other worlds than these"
Stephen King – The Dark Tower